www.bygina.com

ISBN 978-1-7331073-0-3
EAN 9-781733-107303

First Edition: May 2019

A Mirror and A Prayer

A Mirror and A Prayer
The Gina Rivera Story

An Autobiography

Written by Gina Rivera
with Gabrielle Denise Pina

For Jason

My beloved husband, you continually motivate and inspire me everyday. You make me a better person and encourage me with your undying support. Thank you for being my best friend, love of my life and my rock.

Table of Contents

"Romans 12:2 – Do not conform to the pattern of this world but be transformed by the renewing of your mind. Then you will be able to test and approve what God's will is – his good, pleasing and perfect will."

"Be the example you want to see in others."

This means establishing high standards for yourself as a leader.

Don't expect anyone to follow you if you don't practice what you preach.

Maintain high expectations for what you want to accomplish.

Be humble and appreciate those that have joined you in creating the culture. If you can do these things, you are well on your way.

Noted novelist and philosopher Ayn Rand once said, "The question isn't who is going to let me, but who is going to stop me?" This particular quote summarizes the indomitable spirit of one Gina Lee Rivera. Most people come into the world not knowing who they are or what they are supposed to do with the talents that they were given. Some discern their purpose in life in due time; some are not that fortunate and waste precious years walking through doors destined for someone else. Some dabble over decades until life forces them to remain steadfast in an appropriate direction for the evolution of their own soul, and some come out of the womb with a feisty disposition, a humble heart, and a plan. Such was the journey for Gina Rivera, Founder and President of Phenix Salon Suites, a multi-national award-winning franchise chain. From the moment her feet hit the ground, she had something to prove, she demanded to have her say and elucidate her vision, no matter the consequences. Nothing or no one could stop Gina from being Gina, much to her parents' chagrin. This obstinate constitution, of course, invited challenges and quagmires, but she prevailed with her spirit intact and followed her own path until she arrived at her destination. This stubborn little girl, wide-eyed and precocious, wasn't viewed as capable or as a leader, decided to change the only game she knew, the game that warmed her blood. She heeded the call and, in turn, changed the game itself. Gina, along with her husband CEO Jason Rivera, have created a pathway to success, entrepreneurship, and financial independence for thousands of salon professions who occupy their suites.

With over 250 national locations to her credit and plans for international expansion in Europe, a thriving product line By Gina, a series of articles enjoyed by thousands, two television series in development, and a loving and supportive family to sustain her, Gina Rivera has effectively and irrevocably become a formidable force in the global beauty industry and the face of one of the fastest growing franchises in the nation.

Gina's pathway to success took its toll in many ways, yet her commitment to herself, to her values, and to her family has never wavered. In spite of crushing losses, unexpected obstacles, and the occasional bar fight in her roaring twenties, she has persevered and evolved to create a three-dimensional life that few could imagine. As the youngest child of Larry and Janice Peneschi, stylists themselves, Gina began her journey by sweeping up hair in her parent's bustling salon. Instead of being the typical kid forced to work in her father's business, she listened and learned and fought to implement what she absorbed at every turn. Gina found meaning in every snip of the scissors, every whirl of the dryer, and she immersed herself in the pages of various magazines. Songs played overhead became inspiration and the familiar aromas of the shop became a comfort. The atmosphere spoke of possibilities and transformation.

The young girl could have ignored her creativity and vision and simply followed the blue print laid out before her but that wasn't enough for the aspiring mogul. No, this was not only about possibilities and transformation for patrons, but the enterprise itself. Her goal was a singular one, to do better, to be better, to grow into the woman her mother Janice raised her to be and to become the faith-filled woman her God would be proud to know.

The goal remains the same, and so, maintaining the status quo and settling into successful mediocrity, if there is such a thing, has never been enough for this beauty icon. Ms. Rivera does not believe in standing still or resting on her many laudable accomplishments. Poised and coiffed, she glides forward to new and innovative challenges and opportunities. The journey can be dizzying. Some of the challenges and opportunities terrify her, but she has never allowed fear of the unknown to cripple her ambitions or lure her into a direction she knew she had no business going. Steadfast and focused, Gina Rivera is determined to create an empire and an enduring legacy, and not just for her children Phenix and Priest, but for any woman who refuses to do as she's told and dares to dream her own dreams.

There is something quite intriguing about a woman whose spirit defies convention and dares to learn and live on her own terms. Conventional society dictates that women are supposed to follow certain pre-determined rules and behave in accordance with societal gender norms. Well, this woman, who hails from generations of hairstylists, barbers, and beauty professionals, developed her own rules with unmitigated style, a sense of purpose, and a conviction to lead by example. Her kind of meteoric success cannot be quantified by mere analysis as it requires coloring outside of the proverbial lines, failing and having the courage to fail again, and never allowing anyone to rewrite or repurpose the very rules she designed for herself. How does a woman build a multi-million-dollar company juggling a husband, a job, and a family all while strutting about town like Aphrodite with a blond mohawk in Gucci shoes? Carefully, Gina Rivera would say, very carefully and with an abundance of love, dedication, and commitment to do what her internal compass guides her to do, as it hasn't failed her yet.

This autobiography illuminates the life of Gina Rivera, the amazing highs and the devastating lows, the lessons both painful and beneficial. It highlights her quest for success in a male dominated industry. This work will also afford you the opportunity to share in the wisdom that she's learned while building a vastly successful enterprise. It is an amalgamation of sorts, one-part narrative, one part how to succeed in business and the rest is all inspiration. Gina Rivera's story is meant to empower, inspire, and encourage other women to push through their own fears and doubts in order to live their best lives with passion, humility, and enthusiasm. In the end, in spite of the myriad of obstacles placed in her path, in spite of her own self-doubt, and with a devoted heart to be the best that she could possibly be, Gina Rivera too pushed through every single door meant for her to open, and she's only just getting started.

GDP

Dearest Reader,

Like many things in my life that I've been asked to do, I've balked, protested, and wondered why I was even asked in the first place. Writing this book was no different. When my husband, Jason, suggested that I write an autobiography I told him that he was nuts but I've told him that often in our marriage so he ought to be accustomed to it by now. I've been way off the mark most of the time. He has seen strength in me that I haven't always seen in myself and for that I am eternally grateful. I mean what's the point of even having a partner if he or she can't make you better, can't see the greatness in you, and can't encourage you to push past your own fears and insecurities? After I agreed to pen this book about my life, I had no idea what would happen, what would be revealed, or what it would be like to have my live splayed out on the page for all to read. Being on Undercover Boss was nothing compared to this! I frankly didn't think that my life was all that interesting but the folks around me begged to differ.

This book is an accounting of my journey thus far and as such I've included my own brand of wisdom that I hope and believe will be helpful and inspirational to you as the reader. So, there are quirky antidotes, quotes and tips on how to succeed in business and in life. My goal here is to motivate, educate, and inspire you to pursue what is beckoning you to follow your passions and to experience the fruit of your labor with grace and integrity. I hope that my journey can influence yours in a positive way. I hope that you realize that life is meant to be lived and experienced in colour. I hope that you begin to recognize your own truth, and I hope you begin to see the greatness in yourself. Most importantly, I hope you understand after reading my story that obstacles don't have to halt your dreams and mistakes don't have to define you for the rest of your life. You define you. You are the difference and the heroine in your own story.

Life is a do over, my friends, and things can and will always change for the better if you work hard and allow your vison to take root and blossom. If there is one thing that I'd like you to take away from my experience, it is this in a nutshell…If a path does not exist for you, then step off of the path you are on and create for yourself, one that is distinctly yours. You know you better than anyone else, so keep your head up, nurture your dreams with dedication and hard work, and success will be there waiting to welcome you home.

Blessings always,

Gina

"Staying positive, motivated, and productive is directly related to being thankful. Prioritizing thankfulness on a regular basis is the right thing to do. If you do it regularly, it will boost your business in ways you could never imagine."

"Nourishing routines create structure and structure results in discipline. Discipline is absolutely essential to have if your desire is to become successful."

Develop solid routines that ground you.

Spiritual food, like morning devotionals and daily prayers, can give you strength, focus, and determination in preparation for the day ahead.

Stay the course, meaning be consistent.

Create a positive thought process from the time you open your eyes.

Your body is its own mechanism and you must take care of it. So, eat a nutritious breakfast, take medication that your doctor has recommended for the morning, stretch, maybe do yoga or a short workout. Take care of your body, remember, it's the only one you will ever have.

Finally, review your daily planner. Take an inventory of the day that is ahead of you.

"Philippians 4:19– And my God will meet all your needs according to the riches of his Glory in Christ Jesus."

Reflect on those who have had a positive impact on you. Always thank people face to face, if possible.

Handwritten, personalized, thank you notes are engaging and authentic!

If you own a business, be sure to also include a gratitude message on your social media platforms.

Don't forget to thank those who have mentored you as well.

"Take time to identify distractions, prioritize work, create schedules and allow time to gather your thoughts each day. It may seem basic and simple, but I guarantee that you will accomplish more and eliminate distractions from creeping into your mind. So, get ready to focus and accomplish your goals!"

Five Rivera Rules

First, having pride in yourself and your work is key in order to build a successful business.

Second, take pride in your appearance and look your best when taking care of clients.

Third, keep your work environment clean. Remember, appearance is everything and your work space represents how you respect and operate your business.

Fourth, prepare the evening prior for the next day. This will help you to put your best foot forward at the start of each day.

Fifth, and finally, always be on time and ready to go. Timeliness is a clear way of stating that you have pride and others are important.

"Psalms 40; 2-3 – He lifted me out of the slimy pit, out of the mud and mire; he set my feet on a rock and gave me a firm place to stand."

Setbacks can be healthy because they drive you to be the best you can be. You are always better once you have overcome a setback. Face your setbacks as they come your way and you will continue to grow and build a successful business as well as a successful life. A dream that almost died due to a setback is now a growing national brand.

Learn to face setbacks in a meaningful way that have a positive impact in the long run.

Vow to change your attitude and persevere.

Maintain focus.

Most importantly, during this time cultivate an 'attitude of gratitude.' Take just a couple minutes and reflect on the things you are thankful for.

Chapter 1

The time-honored maxim that fruit doesn't fall far from the tree is more than appropriate when examining my life. Gabrielle was far too kind with that awe-inspiring introduction of me and the whole path of purpose set for me from the start declaration (I get a lump in my throat and want to meet this chick she's talking about every time I read it). At the same time, she may be more insightful when I reflect further. Although I explored many other professions and lived different kinds of lives i.e., an event planner, Olympic ice skater, or a saucy yet aloof bartender, hairstyling was indeed etched in my DNA whether I wanted it to be there or not.

I'm sure some of you can relate to having something stalk you until you finally turn around and either A. kick the shit out of it or B. ultimately embrace it. Oh yes, even as I dabbled here and there, "saloning" coursed through me, forever whispering which direction to take and reminding me every day just who I really was. It forced me right when I wanted to go left, and it pulsed through my veins creating an undeniable and addictive rhythm. Look, I tried to run from my birthright a time or two, but the notion of hair follicles, creamy botanical enriched conditioners, and curated color haunted me and wooed me like an annoying ex-boyfriend with a bowl cut until I surrendered to the only life I knew. Hailing from generations of coiffed hair professionals fueled me with a certain inherited confidence and inspired me to jump into that warm and comforting pool of familiarity with both feet and no life vest. Hair has been the foundation of my family's livelihood for nearly a century. I mean, in my world, what else was there? So yes, I went into the family business, into a path that had already been laid out by generations before me. By doing so, there were still more challenges than I could have imagined.

I was born on July 30, 1970 to Janice and Larry Peneschi in the Texas Panhandle. Yes, Amarillo, home to Cadillac Ranch and the historic Route 66! And, being the youngest of two from my mother, I was raised in the quintessential Italian American family complete with animated pasta nights, the proverbial white picket fence, and a thriving family business; however as in every family across the world, there were trials and tribulations, animated debates, and moments of sheer emotional exhaustion. My parents sold their house in Amarillo in 1973 when I was three and made the impulsive decision to relocate. My mom took my sibling and me to visit her parents in Colorado Springs and decided right then and there that she was not stepping another foot in Amarillo again. My dad had no choice but to pack it on up and join us at the eastern foot of the Rocky mountains where we were already enjoying iconic red sandstone formations and breathtaking mountain views.

We settled in Colorado Springs, and my mom stayed at home with me for a time before eventually going to beauty school herself approximately eight years later. My dad exceled easily enough at the one thing he did best, styling hair.

He became a hair stylist thus following in his sister's family's footsteps and he opened Scissors Hair Designs. Soon enough, he began to make a name for himself. Everybody (and I mean everybody) wanted to go to Larry and soon enough life was good, the bills were paid. My father's thick, luxurious, and perfectly cut black hair, as well as his stylistic prowess in the salon became a thing of legend. As expected, he attracted an amazing clientele, boasted a natural rapport with the ladies, and kept his services booked out well in advance. I inhaled the sudden excitement he generated, and I was in awe of the way the women floated out of the salon, quick to greet anyone they crossed paths with as if in a hurry to introduce this new version of themselves. My respect for his talent grew as I learned what it took to achieve such mastery. I remember hearing stories about how my dad used to stay up all night smoking cigarettes and perfecting his craft for those competitions before I was born. He was obsessed with hair, my aunts said. He wanted to be the best. Coming in

second was not an option. He had advanced from winning hair competitions back in the day with his family to now owning and operating his own thriving salon. From as early as I can recall, he worked twelve hours a day and six days a week until his back and feet ached. Exhaustion? What was that? He was driven to exceed his own expectations behind the chair. I know now that I owe my dogged determination and my willingness to always be better to my father.

The move to Colorado seemed to work out. I was blessed to have two parents and extended family, a successful family owned business, and regular ski trips at least three time a month to Copper Mountain, Vail, and the Keystone beginning when I was four years old. I would spend time in the summers with my Aunt Pricilla, my dad's sister, and my cousins. Those were good times and I have many fond memories of our shenanigans. Even then at so young an age, when away from the salon, I would imagine my father working his magic.

I remember sitting in the salon watching my father work and then daydreaming longingly into the nearby mirror. One day, that's going to be me, I thought, one day. From the outside, we had, for all intents and purposes, what many in America yearned for and worked hard to attain; a complete family, consistent income, and the blessings of business and home ownership, but in life things aren't always what they seem. Smiles can abound during the most challenging of times. Resentments fester. Walls can be built in a house full of love and laughter. While my dad built a business from the ground up, honed his techniques, and amassed quite a following in the community, life at home began to suffer.

My family began to transition into something foreign

and unfamiliar, one misunderstanding at a time. They began to argue more than usual, about money or too much time spent in the salon, anything seemed to put them at odds. Parents have rough patches, kids know and can usually time when things will blow over. This was different, like a cloud of pungent hairspray that hung in midair and refused to dissipate.

As the arguing and discord continued, I often wondered if divorce was in their future and if they too were going to become a statistic. I, especially, worried that my house was eventually going to catch on fire from my parents' incessant verbal fisticuffs. The sparks between my parents had often led to smoke, harsh words, and recriminations, and in my young mind, smoke always leads to fire. A fire would mean two separate houses, horrid wart-having step-parents, more discord, less vacations, and a loss of everything that I held dear. I was attending a private Christian school at the time, and I didn't want anyone to know what was going on at home. Everyone else there seemed so perfect and I felt out of place. I know now that that was nonsense as all kinds of families have challenges. Still, this revolving and panic laced thought contributed to many a sleepless night and stoked my ten-year old anxiety. I nearly worried myself to a nervous breakdown (but more on my self-induced breakdowns later).

Frankly, during the 1980s approximately one in two marriages in the United States ended in divorce. This statistic was a reflection of changing lifestyles, divorce laws, and other mitigating factors, so my worries were not unfounded

(I just had to put that out there). Still after repetitive rounds of contentious discussions, door-slamming, and name-calling, my mom and dad managed not to completely unravel and to keep us somewhat intact. To fully comprehend how I became the woman I am today, one has to understand the foundation of my beginnings, the complex family dynamics, and the sheer love that bound my family through triumph and heartbreak.

In 1969, my mother was expecting a baby. From what I've learned, she was excited and anxious for the new arrival. Babies always made things better, and a part of her probably yearned for a shift in focus. When she was approximately six months pregnant, she was standing on a ladder placing something in the cabinet when all of a sudden she tumbled downward crashing to the floor below with nothing to break her fall, and as result she lost the baby and the chance to renew her family. Family accounts indicate that she was so bereft at the unexpected loss of her little one and so furious that she began to blame everyone, including my father. This resulted in countless arguments between my parents. Now, we've never discussed this as a family, but I believe that this singular event deeply impacted the traditional mother-daughter bond between myself and my mother. A short time later, my mother became pregnant with me and my birth slowly started to assuage her pain. Our bond was a strong one. It still is to this day.

"Focusing your energy in the right areas is very important if you want to be successful."

Building a business is not a sprint, it's a marathon.

It is okay to be in a hurry to reach your goals; however, endeavor to remain patient, diligent, and disciplined.

Set small goals and establish a time line for yourself.

Make an outline for your project that includes a written draft plan and a loose timeline. Remember that situations may change so allow your plan and timeline to be modified in case you need to add in new items or eliminate unnecessary items.

Flexibility is key when pursuing new endeavors.

Keep in mind that we will always have a few mistakes when starting out, but remember, your goal is to create less work for yourself by being prepared.

Be ready to learn through this process.

Be open to new concepts and never develop tunnel vision because you may miss important information or opportunities.

Challenge yourself to see the bigger picture when it comes to success.

View your career as an investment.

Be patient and let it grow.

Chapter 2

According to family lore, I was the only grandchild that my maternal grandmother who we affectionately called Pretty Pearl, had to spank. Pretty Pearl, like many intuitive grandmothers, saw defiance brewing in me from the moment I emerged from the womb, and Lord knows she tried her best to keep it at bay. But, even at a young age, I ached to be heard and needed to be seen for whom I was. I craved control, and I was determined to get my way however I could and whenever I could. I didn't want to be the one waiting to be chosen for games and activities; I wanted to be the one doing the choosing. I admit now that I didn't believe

 that certain people in my family and in my business life thought I was capable of leading or of creating a path for myself. I was not going to accept or conform to other people's expectations of me. I was determined to make a name for myself and be successful. Successful women were passionate, right? And they weren't afraid to take risks. They were adaptable

and tenacious and deep down they believed that they were going to be successful no matter the circumstances. I knew at a young age that I possessed these qualities even if no one else did, so I resolved to prove all of the naysayers wrong. Nobody was going to tell me what I could or couldn't do. My destiny was mine to create and mine alone and that caused my grandmother to get real old school with me, obviously.

My temperament provided some memorable moments with others as well. I remember that I loved the Captain and Tennille, so I asked my dad, while in the first grade, to give me a haircut like Toni Tennille. I am certain that this brilliant idea came to me when I was spinning in circles belting out "Love Will Keep Us Together" in Scissor's Salon. Of course, the famed pageboy haircut ending up resembling a mutated mushroom that hadn't quite bloomed on me. Go figure. I was mortified and decided to wear my favorite fuzzy hat until my hair didn't resemble a colossal hairmare (a nightmare involving your hair, yes I just created a word). I tried in vain to hide at home until my hair grew back into its former glory, but my parents forced me to return to school much to my dismay, shrooom hair and all. I'll just keep a hat on for the rest of the school year, I told myself, but to my utter horror the dreadful Ms. Christensen insisted that I remove the offending fuzzy hat in class and thus began the hair/school drama for little ole me. From that moment on, I loathed school.

School was Lucifer's laboratory; school was the man trying to keep me down. I hated anything to do with it, and I especially detested that Ms. Christensen who clearly demonstrated no compassion for my predicament at all. Every morning without fail, I pleaded with my mother to allow me to stay home. Sometimes my mother acquiesced and sometimes she didn't fall for my manipulations. I attempted a dignified protest on Tuesdays and Thursdays and raised bloody hell Mondays, Wednesdays, and Fridays. On occasion, I raised the stakes when I felt it was necessary. I even threatened to cut my own bangs off once if she didn't let me stay home. She didn't negotiate with me in a timely fashion so I made good on my threat. That's right, I grabbed the scissors and butchered my hair in protest!

I used whatever I could to get out of school, even false claims of sickness that manifested in ways I could not have predicted. Call this an early lesson in speaking things into existence. I wept in grand fashion most mornings and experimented with faking sicknesses with a myriad of stomach ailments hoping that my mom would cave and allow me to stay home and let me day dream in peace. When she did acquiesce, I'd end up eating breakfast with her at (the unfortunately named) Sambo's restaurant instead of suffering through class. Eventually my weekly machinations combined, with my anxiety about attending school, caused a real ulcer. I was officially sick, so Mom had no choice but to take me to the doctor. The doctor relayed to my mom that I liked to be in control, and that I could easily be in control at home. Much to my horror, my mom stopped falling for my daily tantrums and promptly sent me back to school, albeit slowly and with a can-do attitude, or so she thought.

The drama at school began before my shroom haircut. Shy and insecure, I had difficulty making friends from the start. Like many kids my age, I felt I didn't quite fit, so I had trouble connecting to the many personalities around me. I wasn't your typical girl who gossiped over boys and rearranged her outfit twenty times in a day to attract attention. On the contrary, I was maverick who refused to conform to the status quo, much to my parent's chagrin. I had to be my own person in spite of the snarky comments and the lack of meaningful friendships, and I determined to walk my own path even if this meant social isolation and emotional solitude. I worked hard to not attract attention and truth be told I liked being invisible. I was able to absorb information that way, to observe the dynamics and intricacies of my generation and to learn in a way that only I could. As I grew older, I gravitated toward the punk rock kids in school who smoked a lot. I did pick up the nasty habit but hey, I no longer felt so out of place. Those kids saw me and let me blend in the background without any fuss or fanfare. They accepted me for who I was and for a time, I could breathe and navigate through my life like a quasi-normal kid. Here, in this

space, being different was the norm, and I was able to forget about the emotional chaos that still brewed at home, if only for a little while.

The early years for me were filled with worry, worry about who liked me and who didn't. My aversion toward academics formed back then and didn't change at all as I went into school. I still hated school with a passion and to make matters worse, I had started to develop and attracted unwanted attention. I had developed a full figure like my mom and this inspired ridicule, envy, and plenty of pithy comments about my physical appearance. I managed to hold my own in the hallway but navigating through this time in my life wasn't a picnic at all.

Be purposeful. Start by making a list of the items that you are focusing on.

Review the list carefully and determine the items that have the ability to make a positive impact on your life vs a negative impact.

Next, seek out new things that will force you to stretch your abilities and grow your talents.

Don't be afraid to try new things once you find them. Remember, even if you stumble at first, failing can actually be a positive step in the learning process. Work hard on perfecting the new talents that you learn.

Identify the items that you excel the most at and then work to enhance them.

Be bold! Remember, tapping into new potential can be a game changer!

"How you deal with conflicts makes all the difference when it comes to being at peace or being in turmoil."

Review your situation and determine what items can be eliminated to make your life less stressful.

Develop a strategy to deal with conflict because conflicts can weigh you down, stress you out to the max, and suck the life out of you.

Step back and learn to pick your battles.

Prioritize and identify what you really want.

Make a list of the issues that are holding you back emotionally, physically, and otherwise. You will find that some will be easy fixes.

Determine what you are willing to change in an attempt to eliminate the conflict. This may require you to revisit your core values as a person, as a professional, and as a leader. The issues that align closest with your belief system are the ones you need to embrace. The issues that do not align with these values need to be the first on the chopping block to eliminate.

Sometimes this may require giving up some items for others. I had to dig deep inside myself and go back to my core values as a person, a professional, and a leader. This helped me to determine what I needed to give up. The items that aligned the closest with my belief system were items that I knew I needed to keep. The items that did not align were first on the chopping block.

Learn to detach yourself from people who do not support your decisions as trying to please them will not lead to a greater sense of peace for you.

Get your energy and drive back, become empowered and train yourself to evaluate things based on your core values.

Remember to stick close to the values when making decisions.

So, whatever it is that you want to accomplish, start facing your conflicts head on and get rid of as many as possible! You'll be happier for it. And, as I always say, be open to change.

Chapter 3

Life at school became more manageable because I was able to focus on ice skating in addition to sweeping up hair in my dad's salon. The feel of being in the salon felt like  an art gallery and an elegant artist's studio. The welcoming aesthetic was a respite from my life and a place that calmed my frazzled nerves and soothed my anxiety. During this time, I also took ice skating lessons at the Broadmoor in Colorado Springs and fell hopelessly in the love with the sport. Sliding across the ice erased my fears and reminded me that I was talented and capable and strong at something. I managed to release of all of my inhibitions when I skated. My residual tensions melted away into the ice beneath my feet as the rink's cool breeze came over my face with attempts at bunny hops and crossovers. If I trained hard enough, my coach said, I could be the next Dorothy Hamill! Of course, I imagined myself in a bejeweled one piece and that snazzy haircut to match. With vigorous practice, I was convinced that I could make the USA Olympic team and be featured on a Wheaties Box or be in a Sears catalogue. I could wow the world, I mused back then, with camel spins, butterfly jumps, and triple axles! Life as I knew it would never be the same, but, as I could have predicted, the answer from my parents was a resounding no, so I moved on leaving my dreams behind on the ice in the Broadmoor.

With puberty came surliness, migraines, and eventually a goofy looking boy named John and some typical teenage exploration. As expected, John shifted his affections from me to the new girl at school as dumb pimply boys of a certain age tend to do. That same year I had the good fortune of having my appendix removed, which caused my adolescent adventure with the fickle John to fade into oblivion. Next to the pain of having an organ removed and the slow recovery afterward, the pubescent heartache paled in comparison. Just when I thought my heart and my body were on the mend, my family erupted into pandemonium. My older sister fell pregnant with a black man's baby and the house became a warzone as my parents tried to come to terms with what they perceived to be an unacceptable turn of events. It was bad enough that she was unmarried and knocked up as a teenager but to be impregnated by someone whom they would not have chosen, hit a new level of outrage. The constant fighting became intolerable, and I reacted to the situation by filling my mouth with whatever buttery salty carbohydrate was available to me. Food became my therapy, and I counseled myself often resulting in substantial weight gain and low self-esteem. Soon enough, I found myself overweight and no longer socially acceptable in any arena familiar to me. I felt lost and powerless. My new portly body attracted way too much attention and attention was the enemy. I could no longer blend in and merge into background. I was on center stage all of the time whether I wanted to be or not, aching to run but realizing that there was no safe haven. The salon even carried the energy of the discord at home. And, of course, as hard as I tried, I couldn't control the environment at home. No one was listening anymore. Every single thing in my life was spinning of control and I was helpless to stop it.

When I was a sophomore at Air Academy High School in 1985, my counselor pulled me aside and relayed that the Vogue Beauty School, an area beauty school, was offering a highly rated vocational program. Elated at the prospect of transforming my life into something that I could recognize, something that I could feel, I jumped at the opportunity to enroll. I attended regular classes at the high school, left in the middle of the day to attend the beauty school, and then returned to the high school to take my last class of the day. I was living my best life! I loved the hands-on learning and I became more of myself than I had ever been. I could breathe and laugh and just be without feeling estranged from myself. I exceled at my classes, started smoking much to my mother's horror, and began little by little to feel more comfortable in my own skin. This experience ignited my independence and gave me the strength to stand on my own two feet. I was starting to understand who I was, if only for a moment in time. I glimpsed the strength of my spirit and that changed me for the better. I just didn't realize this at the time.

Meanwhile, my sister gave birth to her first child, a boy she named Anthony. Ironically, Anthony's birth seemed to bring the family closer together and tear them apart at the same time for obvious reasons. Still, he was the most loved baby and the first baby boy born in the family in forty-seven years. Everyone dove in to take care of him and to support however they could. Random outbursts and tense tears aside, family is supposed to stick together and that's what we did and that's all there was to it. It was the Peneschi way, after all. I grew close to my adorable nephew, and I loved him so.

Life had changed for our family and I longed to be with my nephew and help out as much as I could. From time to time I socialized on the weekends, indulged in plenty of adult beverages, played Spades, and listened to music at my nephew's dad's house on the other side of town. In truth, I had no business being there but hindsight is twenty-twenty, if you know what I mean. We partied hard back then and we had fun until we didn't. I've never been one to back down from a fight no matter the circumstances, and I'm known to give as good as I get. There have been times when this personality trait has been my undoing. On one of these routine weekend nights when I was still a teenager, I said something jokingly to one of the guys at the gathering. To this day, I don't remember what the hell I said but knowing me and my mouth, it must have packed a wallop. This dude flew across the card table, wrapped his fingers around my neck and squeezed and squeezed! I was beyond scared! I couldn't breathe, and I couldn't fathom that there was a 300-pound man literally trying to kill me. As I began to lose consciousness, folks in the room worked to pry his fingers from around my neck, and I prayed to God to let me live. I remember thinking that I was going to die right there in the middle of a Spades game. It took every person there to free me from his grip as he refused to let go.

Frightened and way too terrified to call the police and press charges for attempted murder, I staggered to the car and drove myself home with tears streaming down my face in the middle of the night. Traumatized with red ligature marks decorating my neck like an unwanted piece of dime store jewelry, I crawled in the bed and wept quietly until I fell into a troubled sleep. I awoke the next morning in pain, pretended that life was still a bowl of cherries, accessorized with scarfs for days, and never mentioned a word about that night to my parents. I knew instinctively that my parents would never let this go, so I hid the truth, ignored the voice in my head that said say something, and resumed the pattern I had been trapped in for years. Several years later, I found out that the same man who tried to end my life that night was serving consecutive life sentences for murder.

"If you're going to be successful in business and life, you must be able to adapt in order to grow."

"Following through on your words and promises is instrumental when growing your business. Clients and professional associates will only develop trust in you after witnessing you fulfilling promises and standing by your word. When you promise something to a client and fail to follow through this can be interpreted as a direct reflection of your character as well as your professional abilities. This is why it is important to follow through on the promises that you make."

Don't make too many promises because in today's world situations can change rapidly and circumstances may prevent you from fulfilling the promises you have made. While occasionally this may happen to all of us, we must remember that people can be somewhat non-forgiving when they have been disappointed by their expectations not being met.

Instead establish clear objectives and communicate your plans for achieving these objectives. This way if you are having challenges achieving your objectives, you don't have to do as much damage control if you fail to meet them. It's easier to explain that you are developing a new strategy rather than failing to fulfill a promise.

This approach allows you to try various methods for reaching your objective without putting yourself under a rigid timeline. This allows for some trials and errors if at first you don't succeed.

If you have to make a promise, make absolutely sure you can keep it. Not only will your clients and business associates feel better about you, you will feel better about yourself!

Chapter 4

The marks on my neck healed, but nothing was the same for me after I was attacked that night. I felt like I was walking around in someone else's skin. The Gina that I had come to know disappeared as quickly as I found her. I went about my days doing what I had always done but now it was if I was going through the motions and I could barely breathe. I felt trapped in a life that no longer belonged to me. After feeling this way for quite some time, I resolved to make some immediate changes in my life. I knew nothing good would come of me if I stayed in Colorado Springs stifled and stagnated, of this I was certain.

My favorite cousin Marchelle, who was a few years older than I, upped and moved to Arizona the previous year. Marchelle was having the time of her life and she also shared that in Arizona one could apprentice in a salon without a high school diploma. It was the sign that I had been waiting for, so it wasn't too long after that initial conversation that I formulated an escape plan. I promptly dropped out of high school, packed a bag, and told my parents that I was going to hang out with Nikki, a friend from school, for a couple of days. I can honestly say that I never once worried about my parents' reaction to my decision nor did I panic. I was Gina Lee Rivera and nobody but nobody was going to tell me what I could and couldn't do. I was saving my own life my own way. I called my grandmother and Pretty Pearl purchased a ticket for me to fly to Scottsdale to meet Marchelle. So, with a spirit full of defiance and determination and twenty dollars in my pocket from Nikki's mother, I blew town in a hurry like a convict in a prison raid! I didn't connect with my parents for a couple of months. I just needed to get my head together without any interference plus I knew that Pretty Pearl had let them know I was still breathing, albeit in another state.

On the plane ride there, I smoked an entire pack of Newport's (this was back when you could light up on planes) like I was on speed on something and counted my blessings. I was grateful that Marchelle was waiting for me and that I would finally have some peace, a calm place to live, and unconditional acceptance. My cousin was more like my sister. She still is, and I knew that I would be safe and protected with her in more ways than one. Marchelle would never leave me to fend for myself, and Marchelle would fight for me. I knew that betrayal of any kind was not an option for her and family meant everything. Marchelle was my safe space and the safe space wanted to protect me. For me, Marchelle was the family member that I leaned toward during difficult times, and this particular cousin represented stability and emotional security. It didn't matter that I didn't have any money or any long-term plan to speak of or any plan at all for that matter. The fact that I was seventeen and without parental guidance or support was of no consequence either. I had Marchelle and for me that was more than enough to make my mark on the world. I was free.

After settling in at the Princess Resort with Marchelle and her friend, I began to exhale again without pain. I enrolled in beauty school. As promised, Marchelle secured a job for me at a salon called Adam's Rib where I apprenticed, prepped hair, prepared trays, worked the books, anything they needed me to do.

The move to Arizona felt more like fate, but there were still setbacks. The owner of Adam's Rib fired me after only six months. I had fallen asleep holding foils while he colored a client's hair. I admit I had partied too hard the night before and my decision to do so had caught up with me. Your heart isn't in the business and you're a slacker, he said with complete confidence. Humbled and horrified, I left and Marchelle left with me in solidarity. You see, she always had my back.

I learned fast from my mistakes and moved on to apprentice for a stylist named Brian at Hair Nuveau, an upscale salon in Scottsdale. Even though he had a serious Napoleonic complex and meandered around the shop with his Great Dane who was larger than he was, I stayed on for a year and a half. While I worked during the day absorbing all of the knowledge that I could store in my brain, Marchelle and I would wild out at night. It's a good thing that this was before cell phones! We were young, single, and we both craved adventure. We rolled a rich drunk for his money once outside of a bar and literally lost the wad of cash five minutes later when the stolen money was stolen from us by an onlooker. Man did we hightail it out of there! We wandered through the supermarket every night without fail and pilfered Nestle Tollhouse cookie dough just for the hell of it, and I admit we managed not to get arrested for stealing gas a time or two. Hey, sometimes a statute of limitations can be a good thing! I know some of you reading this can relate! We entered dance contests at various clubs around town and fought like she devils when the need arose, which was more often than not.

Between getting or giving a bloody nose a time or two and being called dykes due to our extremely short hairdos, Marchelle and I dominated the Scottsdale club scene with a vengeance. On one particular occasion, we sashayed into a club with our edgy hairdos and we were immediately called names and pelted with ice cubes. Well, we scaled the stairs without hesitation and laid waste to every single one of the finger pointing perpetrators. If my memory serves me correctly, it was one epic ass kicking. Growth is good thing, I'm telling you! A cop even admonished me once for kicking a gnarly chick in the chest. I didn't get arrested though because the cop thought I was quite attractive, but then again this could have been Marchelle as both of us were slightly inebriated and neither of us quite remembers who kicked whom that evening. Hey, life comes at you fast sometimes! In spite of the bimonthly bar fights, and the infamous Tollhouse cookie dough shenanigans, we had the time of our lives and made some amazing memories. There were never any heated arguments or uncomfortable misunderstandings. There was no giving more than one could afford to give and no more dysfunctional compensating for the sister left behind. There was only love, laughter, and easy living. Batman and Robin had nothing on us! We were the real dynamic duo but without the money, costumes, and the fancy car!

In spite of being canned from my first job, I felt more capable than I ever had before. I reasoned that I wasn't the first person to get fired and that I wouldn't be the last. One man's ill-informed decision wasn't going to get in my way. No ma'am. The need to comfort myself with unnecessary carbohydrates

vanished, and I could visualize a tangible path forming before me. I was stronger, confident, and gliding ever forward
toward a dream I could feel but couldn't quite yet recognize,
that is until my sister called out of the blue one Tuesday afternoon and announced she was moving to Arizona with the
baby.

"Luke 12: 25-26 – Who of you by worrying can add a single hour to your life since you cannot do this very little thing, why do you worry about the rest?"

Remind yourself that taking new things on may feel un-comfortable at first.

Ward off your inner demons and remember that achievements and greatness rarely arise out of remaining in your comfort zones.

Don't be complacent. Start by selecting your new challenge.

Educate yourself on what you are undertaking. Changes occur regularly in all situations and you must stay on top of those changes. You will be more prepared to adapt if you are educated and able to predict what might be coming down the pipeline.

Take inventory of where you are at, review the information you have gathered, and then outline the steps that will lead you to where you would like to go.

Now, take the first step towards reaching your goal and keep on stepping!

Reflections:

I am often asked the question, "What makes your company different from its competitors?" Well, to be honest, I really try not to pay too much attention to them. I think for the most part, this is a waste of my time as well as my energy which is much better focused on moving my company's affairs forward.

While sometimes it may be interesting to hear what the competition is doing, focus on your own corporate and/or personal obligations. Instead expand your company based on your personal vision. Building a strong corporate culture is a far higher priority.

So, is it ok to do research on other competitors? Sure, but don't let your research consume you or guide your business practices. It will only serve to drain your energy and distract your mind from focusing on important aspects of your own business. Instead, know who you are and what is important to you.

Be aware of the environment that you want to provide and focus on providing it.

Understand how you want a client or associate to feel when they leave your place of business and make that happen. If you do all of these things, I promise you, it won't matter what your competitor is doing because your success will move you to the next level!

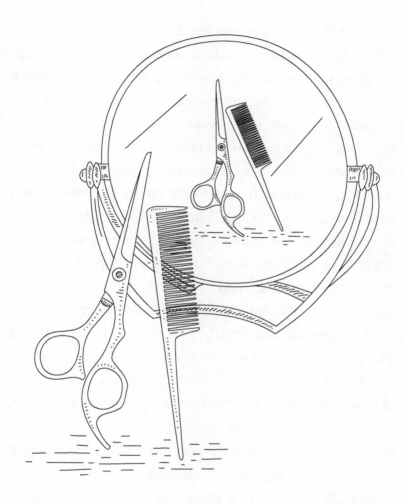

Chapter 5

Just like that, the dynamic duo became a tense trio with a baby in tow and as a result, we decided to move to a bigger place in Phoenix. This new arrangement didn't work out so well for Marchelle, so in time she hightailed it back to Durango. My sister and I scored a job at Bennigan's where she waited tables and I was a hostess. Since she made more money waitressing, I had to remain at home to take care of Anthony, of course. It seemed the only logical solution at time given our dire financial situation. As a single mom with no real income, she qualified for food stamps, and I was often relegated to do the shopping while she worked. I remember a mortifying time when I was at a register with my items and an insensitive cashier announced over the intercom that help was needed to process the food stamps. In what seemed like a flash, my life of adventure and good times in Phoenix had become an abyss of mediocrity and stagnation. While standing there at the register feeling my stomach twisting in knots, I realized that everyone had become the boss of me, a thing that I hated. Now, the path that I had once visualized for myself was beginning to disappear like it had never existed at all. The chokehold of the past returned as the Gina of old started whispering my name, beckoning me back into a life that I'd sworn I left behind.

That sense of heaviness remained in spite of my mom

visiting us a time or two. I ran around like a chicken with its head cut off preparing for her impending arrival. I cleaned and cleaned again. I made sure I removed any remnants of boyfriends or inappropriate engagements. I bought Lysol instead of stealing cookie dough and Clorox instead of Salem's. Truthfully, I made sure there was no incriminating evidence laying around to alarm or upset my mother. As I was still technically under age, any and all indication of alcohol or suspicious behavior had to be removed and scrubbed away post haste. As my mom championed cleanliness, our little apartment had to be up to my mother's standards. It wasn't perfect, but it was the best I could do under the circumstances. I remember feeling nervous yet relieved when I saw my mother pull up in front of the building. I had missed her and I hoped for a peaceful visit. I longed to escape and leave with her, but I just couldn't bring myself to say the words then. My mom stayed a week and made sure that we had food, money, and necessities. Privately, I was heartbroken when she left without me.

Not long after the embarrassing incident at the market, I was working as a hostess at the restaurant and I realized that I wasn't any closer to becoming a real hair stylist. I was busy barely surviving instead of following my dreams. I had an epiphany and I understood that living in Arizona was no longer conducive to my emotional or financial well-being. Now that Marchelle had gone on her own to Durango, what started off as an exciting adventure morphed into this beast that was trying to hold me back and keep me down. Phoenix had now too become another place I had to escape from, another space to wish out of existence. So, I humbled myself and placed a phone call to my parents and begged them to allow me to return home to good old Colorado Springs. I'd even go back to school, I promised, make something of myself, and get my diploma. I wouldn't cause any problems, I told them, and I meant every word of it. I was twenty years old and the time had come for me to turn my life around again.

I promptly settled into my old bedroom and returned to the same high school I had left in such a hurry three years earlier. My father suggested that I just get my GED instead to save face and avoid unnecessary questions and commentary, but I was determined to finish what I had started where I had started it. I was strong and strong women did what they had to do without complaint. Nobody could clean up my mess but me and nobody should have had to. I sat at that desk day after day for a year until I completed every assignment I had missed, took every test, and answered every question asked of me. In the evenings, I concentrated on my homework and continued my training at beauty school. With focus and dedication to my goals, I graduated high school at twenty and less than one year later, I successfully passed my boards at twenty-one. I was a newly licensed professional, and I was well on my way!

"Developing a good business character is so important for success in the beauty industry as well as any profession. Dependability is crucial when it comes to character."

Reflections:

Being responsible plays a huge role in becoming successful. You have to be willing to take ownership for both successes and failures. We all make mistakes when growing our businesses and that's okay and even expected as long as you are willing to recognize your mistakes and work to rectify them. People gain a deeper respect for you when you are willing to take responsibility.

Making mistakes is a part of life. It shows we're human. For me, being in a leadership role, I have noticed that people have a much easier time relating to me when they see me acknowledging my mistakes. Taking responsibility allows me to lead by example in a more effective way. Though at times it can be embarrassing and humbling, mistakes are inevitable but they shouldn't be paralyzing. I say "own the mistakes" because this provides you the opportunity to correct them and ultimately build a successful business and life.

***

First, admit that you have made a mistake and explain how it happened.

Next, assure them that it will not happen again..

Then acknowledge their feelings about the mistake.

Don't down play them whatever you do because this sends the message that the mistake is not important to you and that you don't care.

Finally, let them know that you want to figure out a solution to rectify the error and propose some ideas.

It's important to be open-minded and go the additional mile under these circumstances by allowing them to provide input on the solution. Sometimes this is difficult but it's crucial when moving towards resolving a mistake.

Chapter 6

Soon after I passed my boards, I secured an apprentice position with J Gregory at Viva Salon on the other side of town. I had always admired the man from afar as he was one of the top-rated hairdressers in the area at the time. Viva was THE hot spot; it was where people like me wanted to work. I mean if you worked there, you had to be the shit! I had to bring in a model to cut and style in order to secure a position there. My mom graciously volunteered. With shaking and clammy hands, I cut my mother's hair while Mr. Gregory watched. In spite of my nervousness, I managed to remain centered and calm because my mom whispered words of solace and comfort. "Take a deep breath and slow down," she said. "You know what you are doing," she continued. "You are just as good as they are, and make sure you get my hair really dry." I knew that I wasn't as sharp as my counterparts in that salon but in that moment, my mom made me feel like I was the best hairdresser in the world! To this day, when I'm down or nervous about something, I can still hear her voice quietly cheering me on and telling me that I am more than enough.

I got the job! I loved the experience and I soaked up as much knowledge as I could, but I soon realized that driving to Viva every day was not a viable option. I didn't have the gas money for the trips and it was simply just too far. I decided that I was ready to establish my own clientele and to do that successfully, I needed to work from a salon closer to home. My dad advised me to find a job in a bustling salon so that I could sharpen my skills and build my client base. By this time, he had sold his shop and was working in another salon himself. He was getting older and he was tired of managing employees and stressing over the monthly responsibilities of owning a shop. He liked being able to keep his clientele and go home at a decent hour without the headaches.

I got a job at Joslyn's Salon as a hair stylist for two years and waited tables at Red Robin in the evenings to make extra money. I bought my dad's Mazda 232 in 1993 and rented a two-bedroom condo shortly thereafter. For fun, my girl-friends and I frequented the night club scene nearly every night after work in Colorado Springs. As we were all on limited budgets, we knew which club featured ladies' night with free drinks and which clubs had the best happy hour in town. I worked hard and I played hard as I did in Phoenix, sometimes too hard. That hadn't changed. I remember dab-bling with cocaine a time or two in the ladies' room. Fortu-nately for me, I didn't become addicted, and I was able to walk away in one piece. During one of these outings, I met a man named Aron, and we dated for a time. He was cool enough, but to be honest, the relationship became boring and uneventful, and I accepted that we were both moving in dif-ferent directions. He continued on in the military and I kept cutting hair and partying every chance I got. The path, my path, was starting to rematerialize and I finally felt like my life was back on the right track. The path was reappearing and my sense of self-worth was restored.

Just when I thought I was moving forward in my career as a stylist, the pinch-faced manager at Joslyn's, a woman, said "You don't have what it takes to make it in this business," with the same conviction of the manager of Adam's Rib. I stammered for a response, but nothing came out. "You should find another profession." It annoyed me but didn't break me. The woman probably thought that her harsh words would deter me or maybe even break me, but she had no idea that her misinformed assessment of my capabilities only served to steel my resolve and propel me forward. I knew that she didn't know what the hell she was talking about and besides, I was accustomed being underestimated. If I had folded every time some naysayer told me that I couldn't accomplish something, I wouldn't be able to stand up straight. So, I allowed those poisonous words to roll off my shoulder and land smack on the floor with the remnants of hair that needed to be swept and discarded into the nearest trash receptacle. Instead of giving the woman the satisfaction of leaving right away, I stayed on an additional two months and quit right after I had recorded all of my client's information. My dad did not raise a fool.

With my stint at Joslyn's over, I rented a booth at Columbine's Coiffers where my father worked for about a year. This was the first time that my father and I worked in the same shop, and I loved every minute of this experience. Columbine's was an older salon and it boasted an older clientele and although I appreciated the owner allowing me to work there, I knew that I needed to be around more people my age to be able to attract younger hipper clients. I still have fond memories of Columbine's though because it was one of the first salons where I ever worked and the owner was always accommodating whenever my dad or I needed to rent a booth.

Well, with new-found confidence in my skills, a cadre full of clients, and a renewed sense of self, my dad and I left Columbine's Coiffers together and rented two booths at Illusions, an up and coming Salon up north. I had an abundance of fun, I continued to bond with my dad, and I began to make a name for myself. Imagine that! I was focused and driven and all I wanted to do was work. I worked six days a

week, ten to twelve hours a day without fail. I had no intention of ever being broke again. Plus, I wasn't only supporting myself; I wanted to make sure that Anthony had everything that he needed, and I wanted to be in a position to help my family out whenever the need arose because I knew it would. I was a well-oiled cutting machine, and my clientele doubled in no time at all. I soon earned enough money to pay for the things that I needed. I was completely independent, and that made me feel really good. I was adulting, although that wasn't a term back then! Now, I was in a position to move into my own apartment and rededicate myself to personal goals and aspirations, so I did. I moved into my first beautiful apartment and bought myself a green Eclipse. I was styling, let me tell you! I was flush with cash, and I felt good about my choices, (well some of my choices anyway). Up until this point, I had a thing for a certain type of guy. I was attracted to power and the scope or the morality of the power wasn't necessarily important to me.

I dated this guy named Ricky (not his real name) when I was in my early twenties. Ricky was smooth and strong and quite attractive. He was in the military and he had his life together, or so I thought. I fell head over heels in love with this man like a love-sick teenager. I just knew that this was the man for me, my future husband and the father of my children. One night, he snuck me into the barracks at Fort Carson and the next thing I knew I was face to face with his lieutenant who told me in no uncertain terms that I had to leave right then and there. I did and shortly thereafter, Ricky was dishonorably discharged. He returned home to Detroit and promised that he'd come back for me. I was so gone that in my insanity, I promised to wait for him. While I waited for his return, he was shot, so I had to wait a little longer.

One would think that I would have caught a clue after the bullet thing, but I was glutton for a certain kind of punishment back then. To me at that time any power was good power, and I was hopelessly addicted. Well, eventually he did return to Colorado Springs for a visit and he brought along some friends with him, friends that were reminiscent of another time in my life. These men weren't like his other friends from the military. They were hard, intense, and they sold drugs for a living just like Ricky, I learned. He was making a lot of money, and I was more attracted to him than ever. He and his crew sold narcotics to high-end clientele all over the city, doctors, lawyers, and athletes etc. It was a major operation, and I was the girlfriend of a kingpin! As you can imagine, his business was dangerous indeed, but he did a good job of keeping me far away from his illegal affairs. My mom begged me to end the relationship. She knew heartache was waiting for me, but I waffled because I adored him so. As it turned out, he was under surveillance by the Colorado Police Department and the FBI. I did wonder for a while about the helicopters that always seemed to be around when he visited. I know. I know! Blessedly, he left for Detroit and never returned for me. The last I heard he was serving a life sentence. I dodged a bullet there! I thank God every day that I only wasted a year on that one. There were other romantic missteps that were a waste of my time, but that one was the most interesting.

My professional life was going well, yet my personal life was an unmitigated train wreck. Emotionally and spiritually, I was going nowhere fast barreling toward a kind of self -imposed destruction. I was doing too much with the wrong people. The unbalanced unhealthy life that I was leading was exhausting and had begun to take its toll. Hell, I was walking around like I was strung out at this point. Something had to give. I checked in on my little nephew when I could, tried my best to avoid the ensuing family conflicts, and kept my eye on the proverbial ball. I bought furniture for my new place and I began to move on from the life I once knew as much as I was able to. I was stronger, saying no had become easier, and I was busier than I had ever been at work. I was finally high on my own life for a change, and I liked the feeling of near emotional weightlessness. Success instead of co-dependency had become my new drug of choice, and I was my own damn dealer! The power that I now felt building inside of me was way more seductive than almost any man. I was twenty-five, had clients to cut and style, things to do, and a man to meet. It was 1995, I was in my flow, and little did I know that life for me was about to change forever.

Stay on schedule and show up on time!

Stand behind your work. (Hint: this means if you make a mistake, you ensure it is corrected.)

Know what your brand is and make sure you represent it.

Maintain a level of consistency, i.e.; Relocate only if necessary and make changes only for the purpose of improving your services. Be a reliable source of information in your industry and area of expertise.

Be well equipped with the tools of your trade.

Always conduct and present yourself as a professional.

Maintain a positive attitude regardless of the circumstance.

You're going to be great! Follow these rules and you can depend on it!

"14: 6-7– I am the way and the truth and life. No one comes to the Father except through me. If you really know me, you will know my Father as well. From now on, you do know him and have seen him."

"Listening to your intuition is key when making big decisions and know that there will be plenty of times when your intellect and intuition don't agree. Some ideas that sound wonderful at the time might not be the best for you in the long run."

Step back, evaluate and take time with decisions.

Think long term and picture what the outcome will be a year down the road.

Consider all of the items that the decision will effect; your family, personal life, finances and business.

Take time spiritually to reflect on the decision; pray or meditate depending on your beliefs.

Once you have taken time to do these things, listen to what you are hearing and feeling internally. Then, most importantly, follow it.

Remember, trust what you are feeling, most of the time it won't steer you wrong.

Chapter 7

One balmy June evening, my friends and I visited a bar called Bakers Street to partake in our usual delights, dancing, cocktails, and eyeballing cute guys. I wasn't really looking, but I was paying attention if that makes sense at all. Things were different now though. My friends and I were on our best working girl behavior. We were working steady jobs, and I had matured to that level. Gone were the days of rolling drunks, stealing gas, or planning cookie dough heists for the hell of it! I was nursing my vodka and soda while

engaging in mindless conversation with the bartender when I noticed this fine guy on the other side of the room. He didn't see me, but I was affected by him. I wanted to say something, but I had a boyfriend at the time and plus I couldn't possibly approach a man. My mother would not approve!

Guys chased me. I didn't chase guys! Ever! That would go against a lifetime of Peneschi teaching! In spite of all of my conflicting emotions, along with the persistent voice in my head pleading with me to sit down and shut the hell up, I sauntered in his direction. (God, his eyes were so beautiful, but I digress).

"Excuse me," I said with manufactured confidence fueled by liquid courage. He turned in my direction. "You are so damn hot!" I continued. "If I didn't have a boyfriend, I'd take you out." He blinked and looked stunned by my assertiveness. I turned around, made a beeline for the restroom, and left the bar faster than a convict in a prison raid, let me tell you. I was embarrassed and mortified by my own impulsive behavior. Who was this Gina hitting on a random guy like some common trollop, in a public place no less? My mother would have been horrified! Jesus! It was settled. I was sure I was going to hell.

Around two weeks later, my girlfriends and I were lounging at the bar in Crocodile Rocks, and I begin to gush about this tasty morsel that I had met earlier in the month. I couldn't stop thinking about him, I confessed, the way he walked, the soulfulness in his eyes, the ways I felt when I was with him, even if it was a few moments. I was captivated, I said, by a man that I would probably never see again, and I hadn't even had that much to drink! As fate would have it, in the surreal twists of all twists, and unbeknownst to me, Mr. Soulful Eyes was sitting on the other side of the bar! I swear! Man, I blinked so hard, made eye contact, and shook my head in disbelief. What were the odds? Eventually, we both ended up on the floor dancing to "This Is How We Do It" by Montell Jordan. Go figure!

We ended up talking in a quiet corner for the remainder of the evening. He told me his name was Jason, Jason Rivera. It felt good saying it, and I replayed his name in my mind as we talked. Something passed between us that night, something tangible. I felt it swirling in the pit of my stomach, and I suspected that there was more to come. We exchanged information right then and there. He walked me to my car, and I marveled at how safe I felt with this man that I hardly knew. I had no choice but to give Jason my number. I think we both accepted that our meeting again was more than a coincidence. For me, in that moment, there was no one else in the bar, not the patrons, not my friends. It was just Jason and I creating a moment, and unbeknownst to us, planning a multi-faceted life.

We went on our first date at this restaurant called Manhattan's and we had a great time. I was still technically with the other guy (shall remain nameless), but he was never around because of his job, and we had been heading in different directions for quite some time. He just hadn't been around for me to break up with him in person. On our third date, Jason and I had dinner at a TGI Fridays and in walked my then boyfriend! I could have died right there. Luckily, he or his friends didn't see me, but I was a nervous wreck the entire time. I ended it with him that night and focused on Jason, who turned out to be a gentleman in every sense of the word. He didn't want anything from me that he himself was not willing to give. From that day on, we were inseparable. Dates and shared holidays with both families ensued, a Christmas here and a Thanksgiving there. He was kind and focused, disciplined and determined. He knew how to work hard, and he had dreams, big dreams. He was everything that I ever wanted and everything that I didn't know I needed. He was, I decided very early on in our relationship, the one.

My Jason was confident without being conceited, and he exuded calmness and stability. Perhaps it was because he had been practicing Judo since he was five years old and in addition to beginning Judo at five, he rose early every morning to run, jump rope, and exhaust himself with calisthenics. Further, he started wrestling in the sixth grade, competed all throughout high school and won numerous awards and accolades for his skill and dedication to the sport. After turning down multiple scholarship offers for wrestling, he decided to follow his passion to the Olympic Training Center in Colorado Springs. He trained, worked, attended the University of Colorado, and earned his degree there. Jason's father had instilled the benefits of a disciplined life thus he was prepared to leap over whatever obstacle impeded his path. By the time he reached adulthood, he was trained mentally and physically to succeed, to push past any pain and discomfort, to fall and to get back up. I mention this because his willingness to work hard and stay the course is the very foundation of his character. This spoke to me and reminded me of my father's work ethic. He fit me like a jigsaw puzzle piece more than any man ever had. He possessed an authentic power that was fueled by his own will and was not determined or influenced by external factors. If Jason Rivera had nothing at all but his conscience, he'd still be powerful. Real power ended up being the biggest aphrodisiac of them all. Who knew?

The holiday season of 1998 was surprisingly peaceful and drama free. I was getting busier by the minute and my relationship with Jason was getting more and more serious. He invited me to Washington DC to spend Christmas with his family. Although I felt badly about missing out on my mom's famous ham and potatoes, I was excited about moving forward with Jason. As I boarded the plane, I felt all grown up. I was finally doing what I wanted to do and I was loving every minute of it. Even though I thought the plane was going to fall out of the sky with me in it, I settled into my seat and prayed for the best.

I did always hate flying. My sweetie, of course, was calm and collected as he was accustomed to traveling all over the world for Judo competitions. After the plane took off, he immediately excused himself to the lavatory and shortly thereafter a stewardess informed the cabin that a special announcement was forthcoming. I thought for sure that we were all going to die a horrible fiery death, and poor Jason would be incinerated in the toilet while I melted alone, but God had other plans. The next thing I know Jason regaled the audience with how much he adored me and proceeded to propose right then and there! I was excited and mortified at the same time. Everybody was staring at me and I was nervous and flushed. The stewardess told me to push the call button for yes. Although I was beside myself and in desperate need of a cocktail, I managed to press the right button and to everyone's delight, the captain approved of my answer. We were comped champagne for the remainder of the ride and moved up to first class. I couldn't believe it! I loved him. I loved my ring. I loved my life, and I was over the moon. I had no idea that he was going to ask and I couldn't wait to call my entire family and share the exciting news! I subsequently enjoyed my time in DC with Jason's family. Experiencing a different kind of family dynamic was a welcomed change. They didn't argue or yell. No one was cursing anybody out. They just got along without pretense or hesitation, and I was like, wow!

As Jason was preparing for one of the national finals in Judo, I focused on providing superior customer service at work and finding the perfect first house. Everything was coming together and I was beyond excited at the possibilities. I drove Jason to the airport and told him to be careful. Don't break a leg, I remember saying. He admonished me for worrying. He'd been doing this a long time, he reminded me. Then during his final match to win the championship, as he was attempting a throw, his leg became caught in the mat and snapped in two places. He returned home and promptly moved in with me. One surgery, a titanium plate, and seven screws later, he healed slowly for year while I took care of him. We finally found a house that needed a little work and it just so happened that the work was able to be completed before our big day, so we settled in on Bonnie Brae Lane.

After a year of healing and rehab, Jason decided that he wasn't quite done with the sport. He started training again and traveled to Finland to compete. I was a nervous wreck, but when he returned, he announced that he was done with Judo. He seemed to know that he was destined for bigger and better things, so he forged ahead with training other Judo players and coaching high school wrestling. He was determined to create a new path for himself, and I loved that about him. He focused on a new journey and never looked back. He had a woman to marry, and an empire to help build.

On November 6, 1999, I married Jason Rivera at Shove Chapel on the campus of Colorado College, complete with a pipe organ. Our families were thrilled, and my sister Jami was helpful and supportive, so life was moving at a pace that I could easily handle. Since we had depleted our funds purchasing the house, there was no money left over for any

extras. Undeterred, we had a reception at the Embassy Suites and jetted off to Cancun, a honeymoon gift from Jason's Dad. Like many Americans during this time and now, we both worked hard to make ends meet and lived paycheck to paycheck for a while. We discussed starting a family but agreed that we liked our life the way it was, simple and uncomplicated. Jason had bonded with Anthony and our lives were full. I was working hard in the shop like always, and Jason was the president of his own small marketing company. Still, in spite of our earlier discussions about waiting to start a family, I went off the pill and became pregnant with Phenix four months later.

I was still working at Illusions and I was exhausted most of the time and getting larger by the minute. Working there over time had become an unpleasant experience. I was not one to indulge in the usual salon drama, but it was beginning to follow me and I hated that. It just so happened that I went into labor two weeks earlier than expected so I was unable to show up for work on that particular Saturday, the same Saturday that my booth rent was due. As I was in the hospital nursing my newborn Phenix, the salon owner called and inquired as to why I wasn't at work. Jason informed her that I had just given birth. She congratulated us both and then insisted that someone run her rent down to the shop right away so that I wouldn't lose my booth! I knew that this behavior was typical of the salon owner. Still, I had just given birth, so the comment infuriated me to no end.

When Jason hung up the phone, I decided then and there that I was done with that life, working for someone else and putting up with such nonsense. I was no longer going to be a rat rushing around in someone else's cage. Nope. I decided that my professional life as I knew it was a thing of the past. I just didn't feel like most salon owners genuinely cared about their salon professionals and in that moment, I was determined to one day create a different dynamic in my own salon that changed the culture for the better. There had to be another way, a better way to operate a business in a harmonious environment that inspired and encouraged success. This single epiphany changed the trajectory of my life.

"Everything that comes my way, I'm going to say yes I can."

***

Instead of saying I can't, ask yourself "What if?" Change your mind set and watch how your life begins to change before your eyes. Remember that with the words "I Can" your world expands. It's suddenly much bigger and you will begin to achieve things you never ever thought were possible.

Silence your internal voice that tells you that you can't.

Endeavor to make a paradigm shift in your thinking and cease all self- defeating behavior.

Focus on your blessings.

Embrace the opportunities that come your way.

Destructive thoughts can only result in self-defeating behavior.

Remember as a woman thinketh, so she is.

Reflections:

So many of us are sitting back waiting for opportunities to come our way. It's natural. My approach however, is much different. I believe that you must go after things in life or opportunities will pass you by. Opportunities don't just happen, they must be created. Not only do I believe this, I surround myself and hire people in my company that are like-minded.

If you have passion and are willing to commit sweat, blood and tears, then an opportunity is just around the corner. If you live it and breathe it, you can be sure there is an opportunity coming your way. Yes, there will be obstacles everyday but through these you will learn and grow. Trials and tribulations make us stronger and build character. So, what are you waiting for? Go get your opportunity!

If you don't ask, chances are, you don't get answers.

If you want a specific job, promotion, or pay; then you have to go for it.

Create your opportunity by working hard, being on time, completing your work and bringing new ideas to the table.

Surround yourself with like-minded people.

Make it impossible for your work to go unnoticed.

Make yourself irreplaceable.

Create your opportunity! Then ask for the things you want.

Don't get discouraged, remember the backbone of opportunity is persistence.

"Isaiah 41:13– For I am the Lord your God who takes hold of your right hand and says to you, Do not fear; I will help you."

"When you love what you do, your passion, excitement and enthusiasm will come naturally. These three items can be crucial for expanding your business. They can act to attract clients in a way that will carry you very far in life as well as in your profession."

****

Negativity is bad energy and it can be a big turn off.

When you show love in your heart for what you do, people will gravitate towards you. Positive energy, along with hard work, is the perfect recipe for success.

Be patient and strive to be enthusiastic even when you're tired or questioning your path.

Think about why you selected your career, remember the passion you felt at that moment and get excited again.

You will get there soon enough, even if you're at a crawl rather than a walk, so crawl with a great attitude and you will get there before you know it!

And, as I always say...Be Open to Change!

Chapter 8

As fate would have it, a salon became available for purchase a couple of weeks later, and Jason suggested that we go for it and purchase the salon. I wasn't quite ready yet. I was recovering from giving birth and taking care of a newborn. I thought my husband was insane for even suggesting such a risky move, but I needed somewhere to work when my maternity leave was over and I was committed to changing the culture of the industry. So, in 2003, when Phenix was just six weeks old, I took out a line of credit for $30,000 and purchased my very first salon. It was fairly new and it had six chairs. Jason's dad suggested that we christen our business acquisition after our firstborn, hence Phenix Salon was born.

As there were already salon professionals attached to the salon, I hosted a meeting as the new owner and steeled myself for any drama. I was nervous because hairdressers could be a fickle bunch especially when there is a change of ownership, but everything seemed to go well enough. I returned to work determined to make the salon productive and prosperous. I was now in control of my own destiny! I could now write my own rules and influence the culture as I saw fit. It was a daunting task but I was up for the challenge.

After a few weeks, Jason suggested that we have another salon meeting to implement some changes and set some guidelines for operation. I tried to explain to him that this wasn't a wise move. Salon professionals would rather slit their eyeballs out with razor blades than go to salon meetings. "You're crazy," I told him, and "it's too soon to do this," but he wouldn't listen. So, I acquiesced and scheduled the meeting much to my irritation. In less than one week after the meeting, five of our salon professionals walked out without a word. I then asked my ambitious husband if he was ready to listen to me, and he asked me to teach him everything I knew about the business. We were going to make this work, so we put our heads together and moved forward on a much firmer foundation.

When we decided to buy the salon, I never told a soul, not even my former coworkers at my old salon, Illusions. I was committed to running my business with integrity and I didn't believe in recruiting from other salons. I still don't. Of course, my father, Larry the Legend, came and worked in my salon right away. He had always supported me, and this was no different. My work and my reputation would have to be enough to entice and encourage other salon professionals to find me and want to work in my salon. No matter what, I promised myself that I would stay true to my own core values and honor my mission to create a model salon, treat my salon professionals with appreciation and respect, and hold the industry to a higher standard of service. Although Jason and I were stressed about the viability of the salon, failing was not an option. We had made an investment, and we determined to see our investment through to the end.

In time, my faith in myself paid off, and I had to scramble to build more stations to support all of the salon professionals who wanted to work with me. We knocked down a wall, rearranged schedules, and watched as some stylists doubled on booths just so they could be there. People began to book appointments in droves and soon more stylists wanted to work with and for me than I had chairs for. The tide had turned, and it had only taken three years. Naturally, we began to entertain the idea of expanding into the building next door, but it would have required construction that we could not possibly afford.

As we continued searching for another location and planning for expansion, I wondered what it would be like if salon professionals were given the opportunity to own their own businesses and run them however they saw fit. What if they could suddenly become salon owners themselves without the financial burden of owning a shop or without having to deal with the pain in the ass supervisor? What if salon professionals could experience the dream of business ownership the moment they signed a lease? I remembered when my mom worked in a cubicle type space at the Rustic Hills Shopping Center when I was around ten. She used to remark about how interesting the set up was and how lovely it would be if everyone had their own space to decorate. What if people were allowed to express their individuality? Well, I mused, what if stylists could operate in a similar fashion? After ruminating on this notion for a spell and talking to my mom, I decided to customize the building into suites and provide certain services like towel and product delivery, suite features and options. Now this concept was not new by any stretch of the imagination, but I endeavored to do this my way, incorporate my values, and instill my culture and my personality. I was determined to reinvent this concept, pay homage to my mom, and make this journey my own.

I didn't know at the time that my faith in myself and my abilities would revolutionize business ownership as we now know it. I merely hoped though that my desire to make life better for salon professionals would seem plausible to people like me who wanted to experience business ownership without the hassles and the financial burdens of owning a facility that they could not maintain. I knew without a doubt that my idea was valuable and necessary and that I had to be the one to provide the tools for the dream. I shared my vision with my mom and she immediately recognized the potential. We began working on the project together designing the space and discussing the décor of the inaugural location. We chose colors and patterns and we were determined to create a design concept that would last for generations. Excited and anxious to get started changing lives, I shared my ideas with Jason, and he thought it was the dumbest idea ever! It was different, out of left field, and hadn't been done before, but experience had taught him to listen to me. "Trust me," I said, "just trust me." He did, even with reservations, and before we both could take a breath, a bike shop close by moved out overnight freeing up a coveted space.

It was 2007 and we had no idea if the suites would

be leased or if we were going to lose our investment. We prayed and took a leap of faith together, which proved to be advantageous because the business was a success and salon professionals were clamoring for more! We celebrated with dinner and four shots of vodka while marveling in disbelief at our first extensive waiting list. People understood the concept after all and embraced the notion of being their own boss with vigor and enthusiasm.

Jason and I had discussed expanding our family about a year after Phenix was born. We didn't make any definitive decision, but we didn't do anything to prevent a pregnancy either. I stopped taking birth control and nature eventually took its course. I worked up until my delivery and was blessed to deliver Priest, a healthy baby boy, even though there were a few complications. I think God knew that I could not have taken any more tragic news at that point in my life, so Priest came into the world two years after Phenix, in

spite of the knotted cord that was determined to block his air supply. Divine intervention was at work in my life and for that, I remain eternally grateful.

Meanwhile, my relief at the resounding success of

my business instincts was happiness in motion, but my delight was short lived. My mom had not been feeling too well and the family was worried. I thought that maybe my mom just had a bad bug as she had been known to nurse a cold longer than most. She often complained of a stomach ache and seemed to be susceptible to benign maladies. I figured this couldn't be any different, but lately, she complained of back pain and of being tired more often than not. Perhaps, she had tired herself out playing with the boys. She kept the boys for us while we worked and played with them all day at her house, and they loved her for it. She was the best grandmother I could have asked for and she loved those kids more than her own life. Then, the Friday before Thanksgiving, she called me crying and asked if Jason could pick up the boys. She wasn't feeling well, she said. So, Jason picked up the boys and my dad asked me what to do and where to take her. I suggested the hospital because I knew that they would test her for everything under the sun and eventually get to the bottom of her discomfort. He agreed and headed there. I remember telling him that I would meet them there but he said that there was no point since all they would be doing was waiting, so I went to dinner that evening with my family assured that the pain was probably due to my mom's gall-bladder or simply something that a doctor could fix with a nod and a prescription.

I do remember watching an interview earlier that day with Patrick Swayzee as he discussed his ongoing battle with pancreatic cancer. I thought to myself, how awful and painful that must be for him, but as he began to describe his symptoms, I panicked. They sounded all too familiar. Shortly thereafter I received a call from my dad. They had indeed found a mass on my mother's pancreas. I jumped in the car and headed to the hospital. I knew no one could live without a pancreas. I cried all the way there as I made calls to my aunt Judy, my mother's twin sister and Marchelle's mom, and I prayed to God to help me keep it together. My life as I knew it had just shifted and the shift rocked me to my core. Now all the years of fighting didn't seem so horrible. I just wanted more time with my mom.

By the next morning, family was descending on Colorado Springs and I was grateful for the support. No matter what, in a time of crisis, my family pulled together. My dad confirmed my worst fears on a Wednesday afternoon. My mother had, in fact, been diagnosed with stage four pancreatic cancer. I remember crawling in the bed with her and telling her that she was going to be okay. But nothing was okay ever again and on some level we both realized the oncoming pain of our new reality. The American Cancer Society indicated that for all stages of pancreatic cancer combined, the one- year survival rate is only 20%. The odds were not in her favor and our family was devastated as we all had to come to terms with the inevitable. There was no hope, no cure, and my mother was running out of time.

While I was struggling to cope with my mom's diagnosis, I ran my business as best I could, took care of my children and tried to be present for my parents. During this time, Jason and I were served with a lawsuit. Unfortunately, the contractor we hired to customize the building we'd bought the year before didn't pay any of his sub-contractors and those sub-contractors were holding us liable. It was a terrible mess. (After two years of litigation, we claimed victory, but the battle had taken its toll). Still, in the meantime, we pushed ahead and bought a second property in 2008. While the property was being renovated to accommodate thirty-seven suites, the recession hit and suddenly obtaining financing that had come so easily to us before became challenging.

Six months after my mother's diagnosis, when Phenix was six and Priest was three, I invited my parents to move in with us at my sweet husband's suggestion. It seemed the only viable solution under the circumstances. My father needed help taking care of my mom and I needed to be there for her as much as I possibly could. In spite of my focus to my business, my marriage, and my mom, I felt myself being pulled in multiple directions. I was shrinking, and I felt like I was helpless to stop my own impending disappearance. Everything was happening all at once.

Jason had started his marketing company, JC & Associates, back in 1998 from the ground up. He had been working hard to keep the company in the black and support my salon dreams. He got his first big break in 2002 and picked up a major restaurant chain the following year. This contract catapulted his company to a new level and we thought we were moving forward financially. And then the housing crisis happened right around this time and we began losing lines of credit left and right, and we didn't have the capital to continue. JC & Associates lost a million dollars of business in the span of forty-eight hours as contract after contract was cancelled. We didn't know what we were going to do. Jason thought for sure his company was going to go bankrupt. What about his employees? What about our children? How were we going to pay our mortgage or pay the mortgage on the shop?

These were rough times, but we made it through…together. Jason felt badly for a minute, steeled himself for battle, and turned the company around in less than a year. He didn't focus on the setback but rather concentrated on the solution. And even though we managed to rustle up financing to keep our business afloat, the constant stress took its toll on our marriage. We bickered like never before, came up for air, and argued some more. Whose idea was it to buy another building anyway? Didn't we already have enough to do, to plan, to repair? We blamed each other, and we loved each other through the difficult days when it was harrowing to just make to the end of the week.

During the tender moments though, the moments when love was all that mattered, when the children were down and after my mom had been tucked in for the evening, we both admitted that we never thought we would ever open more than one store. We were both amazed at how far we had come and that we hadn't run our business into the ground what with everything that we had going on in our lives. Together we realized that there was still so much to do and more to learn, but we determined that we were up for the challenge. What I can tell you is that choosing the right partner in life has made all of the difference in the world for me. There was never a time when Jason and I weren't in this together. In order to help me build my salon empire and to ensure that I could stay comfortably behind the chair, Jason sold his company in 2009 and joined me full time in the business.

Now, our new property, the one with thirty-seven brand new suites, opened for business in that same year. I found that if I kept busy, I wouldn't splinter and fall apart thinking about life without my mom, so I focused on one task at time and moved to the next and the next and the next. It was all so methodical back then. I took every opportunity to spend time with her and I endeavored to keep her occupied with discussions about the boys and the shop. On my mom's good days, when she would eat, dress, and put on make-up, I breathed sighs of relief and gratefulness. Blessedly, family was always around comforting her at every turn. No one was fighting and wounds were being healed without too much effort. Love permeated our household and that made dealing with the disease a little easier for everyone involved.

In the midst of this personal storm, confusion reigned supreme in my life. There were no defined roles in our marriage with regard to the business as of yet, so I didn't quite know what to make of myself. I never questioned my role in the marriage or the business, I simply completed my tasks when they needed to be completed. Who was supposed to run the shop? Who was supposed to head the business?

There were plenty of times I wanted to quit all together and just give up but I had made a commitment to see this journey through. Still, I knew that I wasn't paying as much attention to the shop as I should have been. People were in my house all of the time so finding time to myself was impossible. I couldn't potty train Priest because I was behind the chair twelve hours a day on average. I was emotionally compromised and I felt guilty for not being able to be and do what was needed for my family. I felt guilty for not spending every moment I had with my mother, but I was beyond grateful that my sister was pulling up the slack. In truth, there were times that I didn't have the energy to feed my own children or to brush the rat's nests out of Priest's hair. I became detached from everything and almost everyone, breathing on autopilot, and walking around in a skinsuit. I felt alone, and my life was spiraling out of control minute by minute and snip by snip. I wasn't physically or emotionally accessible and I didn't know how to fix any of it. It felt like every area of my life was a complete mess and I was much too tired to even begin to facilitate an intervention with myself. There was too much to do and there was no time to focus on me or my needs.

I spent time talking to my mom whenever I could, whenever my mother was able to muster a few words. At my mom's suggestion, I asked plenty of questions, questions about life, questions about recipes and so on. I was on empty, but I refused to complain especially to my mom, who was lying there in pain and dying a little bit every day. Complaining seemed stupid and inappropriate.

On the very last day that I remember speaking to my mom, she looked at me and asked me what was wrong. I hung my head; I didn't even know how to begin to answer that question. My mom said, "I'm glad that you are so busy and that you have babies, shops, and a husband. You have so much life to live and don't you dare let this stop you. Go on now and be you," she continued. I just remember sitting there listening and focusing on her face and her voice and her touch. And then, not too long after this conversation, my beautiful mother followed the light home and although I was prepared for the loss, my mother's death devastated me nevertheless. Still, I wept tears of joy and rejoiced that my mother was with the Lord our God and that she wasn't in any more pain. There would be no more suffering, no more chemo, and no more bad days. In the weeks and months that followed, I grieved along with my family and in my grief I realized that I needed to do something with myself before the mess of my existence pulled me into a sinkhole.

I was determined, once again, to change my life, take full control of my decisions, and breathe a new kind of air. I swore to myself that I would honor my mother's wishes and forge ahead with a renewed sense of dedication and purpose.

A funny thing happened as I took inventory of my life. I did own a few shops. I was a busy woman. I did have the best most supportive husband in the world and the most loving children. I was blessed beyond measure. I looked at myself in the mirror and smiled for the first time in a long time. I saw myself in a new light and in that moment, a transformation of sorts began to take place. I was Gina Lee Rivera, and I had much more to do.

I made it a point of maintaining strong family ties with family, so much so that the subtitle "extended" seemed like an unnecessary category. The memories of feeling lost within all of the family dynamics when I was coming up inspired me to keep a close relationship with my nephew, Anthony. There was no way I was going to let him feel as though he was out on the fringes of everything. I had been there for him since he was a child. We all had, and now that I was married with children of my own, my devotion to him hadn't changed one bit. I maintained that bond and when his little brother Alec was born nearly a decade later my devotion extended to Alec as well. I had taken care of Alec off and on for the majority of his life and with the blessing and support of my husband, I continued to do so, as he was a part of our family. Alec was with us for summers and holidays, and I love him just like I had given birth to him myself. During his freshman year in high school, when my boys were in elementary school, he came to visit Jason and me and refused to return home. There was nothing left for me to do but make the necessary arrangements to assume legal responsibility for my nephew. Life comes at you fast sometimes whether you're ready or not, and none of us are exempt from trials and tribulations. His mother had done her best and now it was time to do mine.

Just as the business expanded, so did my role as a loving facilitator at home by navigating a world unfamiliar to me in many ways. I went from arranging playdates and reading the adventures of Winnie the Pooh to facilitating high school activities, navigating teenage social angst, and endeavoring to raise a young man of color in a way that celebrated whom he was and nurture our family as a whole. All in all, taking care of Alec has been a gift to all of us, and I have no regrets. I have done the best I could by both of my nephews and that sits well with my soul.

Don't be afraid to think outside of the box.

Getting out of your box can be very uncomfortable and downright scary.

Real growth happens when you are the most uncomfortable.

You may miss out on some of the greatest experiences in your life if you stay in the box you created for yourself.

Chapter 9

Now, after my period of self-introspection, I couldn't move fast enough to suit my own agenda. Like I said, your girl was back in control of her life. The suite concept had taken off and I reveled in the opportunity to offer people the chance to create a path for themselves by owning their own business. The look I saw on salon professionals' faces when they realized that they were now in control of their own destinies propelled me forward with newer goals and loftier aspirations. The clouds had parted in my personal life and things were more to my liking. I was no longer allowing everything and everyone to run me and dictate my life. I was on my own schedule.

The lawsuit that had plagued us from a couple of years earlier concluded in our favor. We had spent thirty-five thousand dollars in attorney's fees, and we won a fifty thousand-dollar judgement. For the record, we never saw a dime of that money, but we were beyond relieved that the lawsuit was over and done with. Lawsuits breed valuable lessons, so we learned from our mistakes and moved forward with vigor and excitement.

Undaunted, we began to look for another property to convert in Orlando, Florida. Orlando was one of Jason's favorite places to go with his best friend plus Florida was the home of the Daytona 500! What wasn't there to love about expanding our burgeoning empire in the sunshine state?

Even though I developed a more composed and serene system for navigating through my life and my business, family remained my first priority. I saved time for my husband and children, and I made time to also help take care of my beloved grandmother. Pretty Pearl was her own woman and always had been. She was strong, stubborn, independent and played a mean game of tennis until she was at least eighty-five! She only stopped because running after the ball by then had become too cumbersome. She didn't suffer fools well either and prided herself on living alone and being able to get around town without assistance. Like many seniors during this time of life, Pretty Pearl developed dementia and when I realized that my grandmother needed help, I adjusted my life accordingly and started to spend more time with her. I had just lost mother and I wasn't ready to lose Pretty Pearl too, but I prepared for the inevitable. It was only a matter of time before she became lost and disoriented or I was inundated with calls from the police.

The ebb and flow of life and death had brought about another very stressful time but our family pulled together once again and did what had to be done. For me, there was no other option. Taking care of Pretty Pearl was tantamount to taking care of my mom or myself. I saw myself in my grandmother, her failures and her triumphs, her struggles and her resilience.

Eventually, Pretty Pearl fell and broke her leg and had to convalesce at a rehab center that happened to be half a block from our house! I was elated that my grandmother was now so close. I knew she was safe and well cared for and during this time, I didn't have to worry so much. On Thursdays, I picked her up and took her to lunch, ran her errands, and prepared for the following week's business. During her stay at the rehab center, I managed to convince her to relocate to the Liberty Heights Retirement Home. I was so proud of my accomplishment here, and our family was ecstatic at this development. But, the day the moving company was scheduled to transport Pretty Pearl's belongings to Liberty Heights, my grandmother ordered me to take her straight home. She wanted to be in her own house. She said she wanted to sleep in her own damn bed and be surrounded by the things that gave her a sense of security and comfort. She had already taken care of everything so all of us needed to mind our business and do what we were told to do. At this point, I realized that all she needed was love and attention and I had no choice but to acquiesce and accommodate her wishes. I loved my grandmother dearly, and I wanted her to be happy during the winter of her life. So, the movers unpacked the truck with care, she settled back into her house, and the phone calls from the police resumed shortly thereafter.

Pretty Pearl died on April 9, 2014, approximately five years after my mom transitioned. For me, her passing was the end of an era and the beginning of new one. By this time Jason and I had opened our third facility in Orlando, and in spite of the trials and tribulations going on in our lives, we were eyeing a fourth location much closer to home.

"1 Peter 5: 5-6 – In the same way, you who are younger submit yourselves to your elders. All of you, clothe yourselves with humility toward one another because "God opposes the proud but shows favor to the Humble. "Humble yourselves, therefore, under God's mighty hand, that he may lift you up in due time."

Being kind is not just our moral responsibility, it's also crucial to building relationships. When you treat others kindly, you develop an authentic bond of respect and trust that is impossible to duplicate.

Talent is something to be proud of, but character elevates your game to a whole new level.

Kindness can serve as a gateway to building strong relationships which in the long run can lead to limitless opportunities.

Kindness allows you to plant a seed with others and inspire them to pay your kindness forward.

do to others
as you would
have them do
unto you

- LUKE 6 : 31 -

Chapter 10

In quiet moments, I still longed for my mother and Pretty Pearl. I learned that if I stayed busy, I could tame the sadness that welled up inside me more often than not. If I focused on my husband and my babies, Phenix and Priest, I would recall my mother's words of encouragement and my whole heart would smile at the memory. And, if I closed my eyes real tight, I could still feel my mom and my grandmother's embrace settling my spirit and reminding me, in whispers, who I was and who I am destined to be. At forty-one, I was starting to heal. I was finally comfortable in my own skin, I had made a name for myself, and I had just opened a fourth Phenix Salon Suites in downtown Colorado Springs with

my husband and business partner. We were both excited at being able to expand our business in our h o m e t o w n . People knew us by now and understood our accomplishments.

Our names were on the proverbial map that we had created. So, aside from those quiet moments that caught me by surprise now and then, I was rocking and rolling and life was good.

Before the dust settled on the Colorado Springs store, Jason and I began to discuss opening a fifth location, in California. Our businesses were running smoothly, we were learning the business at record speed, and our infrastructure was sound. It was 2013 and after consultation with our team, we decided to open the fifth location in Encinitas, California. I wasn't completely sold but the deal had been signed so we proceeded. Who was I to stand in the way of more success? Fear was no longer a part of my decision-making process. I quickly became frustrated with the process this time though when I couldn't seem to get the waterfall design right in the facility, so everything became an unmitigated disaster. I spent thousands of dollars trying to fix the waterfall and it was reminiscent of the troubles I encountered opening my very first store. I couldn't get the waterfall right there either! Even though this was our fifth location, I felt like we were starting over. We were in a new state and we were in a better financial position but we were not in a position to lose any money. Still, we arrived at the grand opening with a smile on our faces and a warm handshake for the Hooka Mayor of Encinitas. I returned home, snuggled my babies, and headed straight to work. I worked magic behind the chair three days a week, twelve hours a day with my dad. I had to multi-task and stay focused as I was booked out a year in advance. Now, everybody wanted an appointment with me! With hard work and focus, I had created this reality for myself. My world was changing yet I couldn't seem to snap out of what now felt like bouts of depression. Although, I had five thriving salons under my belt, I was still grieving, and I missed my mom. After all, she had helped me design the salon. She had been there from the very beginning. Without her, nothing felt the same. I just wanted to stop opening salons, get off the Ferris wheel so to speak, and stay safely ensconced behind the chair. My anxiety was beginning to get the best of me, and I didn't know what to do.

In my quiet moments, I remembered that my mom told me that if I changed my hair and took a leap of faith, I could change my life. I could become a new Gina, she said, a Gina that could accomplish anything. Since everything about me and my life internally had shifted, it was time for me to make the external shift as well. I needed my outside to be a direct reflection of my inside. It was time for me to make sense to myself and this required a radical change in my appearance. I wanted a blond mohawk to compliment my fierce boss lady bad ass attitude. The world would see that I was confident and no longer afraid of who I was. It was time to look in the mirror and finally see the authentic me, the me that had always been in there…waiting to break free.

I told Jason, but he wasn't really paying attention at the time. Now that I think about it, I don't think he really believed that I would bleach my hair and shave my head! I booked an appointment with a colleague with no fear or regrets. I walked in that salon one way and I walked out another. I'm a stylist after all, and I'm accustomed to wearing different styles and, of course, dying my hair, but this time was different and I felt it. Little did I know at the time that my blond mohawk would become my official trademark. My cousin saw me the following day and quipped that I had one big set of balls. Well, I decided to take that as a compliment!

In 2014, Jason was approached by a representative of the Emmy award-winning hit show *Undercover Boss*, a popular reality-based series, where high-level executives disguise themselves and take jobs in their own companies. I initially thought that they wanted to feature Jason, but they wanted to feature me! I was horrified at the thought and I could not fathom being in the spotlight that way, let alone be on television. Now, Jason had to convince me to step outside of myself, and plans had to be made. He sensed that this would be a life-changing opportunity for our company and pushed me to conquer my fears and take the leap into prime-time television!

I was beside myself with anxiety. I had no desire to be the main event, no inclination to open myself up to public or private veneration or castigation. My goodness! What would people think of me? What would my family say? All kinds of crazy things, I was sure, like why didn't you ever do any of that for us? That's not the real you. You only did *Undercover Boss* to get famous. I had heard how such projects encourage people to exaggerate themselves for the cameras, that the experience can destroy relationships. What if they asked me to do something that clearly wasn't who I was? What if I became lost in all of the reality show madness? What version of me would anyone believe was authentic? I wanted to do my work in the background, but Jason convinced me that my background days were over. I was now the face of Phenix Salon Suites whether I liked it or not. So, I left my family, allowed myself to be transformed into the comely Ashley, the stay at home mother who used to be a stylist clamoring to get back into the salon industry.

I began filming *Undercover Boss* in April of that same year. I found the experience to be emotionally and physically exhausting and on the plane ride home I was consumed by imaginary condemnation from my family. I met with salon professionals, pretended to be a barber, a manicurist, and I even put in a weave for the first time. Before I knew what was happening, I became lost in the façade of the "fake" Gina, and I flirted hard with depression during the filming. I ached for my husband like crazy. I missed my boys and I missed my real life. The producers allowed me to fly in my cousin Marchelle to calm my nerves and keep me on track to finish the episode. It was the worst thing for me and the best thing simultaneously. When I returned home, I barely spoke for days and it took a little time for me to recalibrate myself, restore my sanity, and answer to my own name. I was Gina all right but some part of me was still Ashley at the same time. I admit that I experienced a bit of a peculiar identity crisis and I didn't like it at all.

There are plenty of stories out there, stories of actors complaining that their films or spots were edited wrong thus ruining the project or the actor's reputation. I worried how the producers of *Undercover Boss* were going to edit the episode. I wondered how I was going to come off. I wondered just how awful I was going to fail in front of all of those people. All I wanted to do was love my husband, mother my children, and protect my company. For the first four to six weeks after filming, I just knew that I had made the biggest mistake of my life and I nearly worried myself into the mental hospital across town. I suffered a mini-breakdown of sorts and it took me about a month to get myself together.

Although the experience had pushed me to new limits, it also broadened my perspectives. It had been weird to go undercover but getting to know my business from the inside out through someone else's eyes and learning about my salon professionals was rewarding in ways that I hadn't quite anticipated. I didn't hear anything for approximately eight months and Jason and I had to wait to find out the air date. It was nerve wracking to say the least! When the airdate was finally announced, the anxiety began all over again and I was helpless to stop the self-induced insanity. No matter how hard Jason tried to convince me that I was going to be fabulous, I prepared to lock myself away in that mental institution until the hype and fanfare was over.

A colleague of ours suggested that we hold a viewing party at a friend's theater in Colorado Springs and so on January 9, 2015, 200 people arrived in style to watch the premiere of my episode of *Undercover Boss*! In spite of my fractured nerves and my desire to down multiple shots of Tito's Handmade Vodka, I actually loved what I saw! Imagine that! As Jason clutched my hand, I felt a sense of relief and pride. I had done my best and my best turned out to be good enough after all, just as it always had been just as it always will be.

The Phenix website crashed immediately after the show aired. Fans remarked all over the internet that it was the best damn episode of *Undercover Boss* that they had ever seen and I received thousands and thousands of emails. Some were appropriately complementary and others were downright embarrassing. People sent me naked photos of themselves and I was propositioned countless times. My dad was so proud of me, my family didn't hate me after all, and I hadn't completely humiliated myself.

So, everything changed after this show aired. I was now a known entity. I was recognized in the mall the day after the episode aired. Jason and I couldn't go to our favorite restaurant without people recognizing me. The world as I knew it became another thing that I had to get used to and, as I said, my new fierce boss lady bad ass mohawk became my signature look.

Never allow yourself to become complacent. Not staying up on your game can cost you big time. Don't fall into the rut of complacency. Being complacent paves a path for you to be lazy and lose your desire to learn.

It's so important to appreciate your talents and make it a priority to sharpen your skills. Take the time to learn new techniques.

Review new ideas that are becoming a trend in your field.

It's extremely important to stay humble and open-minded in order to broaden your knowledge base.

If you aren't learning, you aren't growing. So, continue to learn from anyone and anything that might help you to develop your abilities at a higher level.

Chapter 11

In 2014 my husband told me that my life story could be an inspiration to other people, especially other women. I brushed him off. I genuinely didn't understand what he meant. Yes, we had built a successful business and yes I had been featured on *Undercover Boss* but I didn't believe that I was any different from anyone else, and I still don't. I just know the benefit of hard work, dedication, and having a devoted supportive partner. I also understand how important it is to have a vision and to nurture that vision to fruition. I needed to do something, he said. I needed to share my story. What if my journey could help others on their journey? But who was I to do anything beyond what I was already doing? I couldn't stand up in front of people and talk like that. *Undercover Boss* was a closed set of a few people, not huge crowds. I wasn't a public speaker by any stretch of my imagination. I was just Gina a salon professional and a business owner, but he wouldn't let the idea go. He pushed and pushed. I told him that he was crazy in the head. Hadn't we done enough? Hadn't I said enough? No one needed to see or hear any more from me. He begged to differ. He refused to let it go and I'm so grateful that he was as persistent as he was.

Well, as I continued to dismiss his hairbrained idea about some kind of event or project featuring me again in a public forum, the women who worked with me at the salon began to tell me that I was an inspiration to them, that I helped them see beyond themselves, that they felt like they could do anything because of my accomplishments. These unsolicited revelations were surprising to me and they completely warmed my heart. I was caught completely off guard and I was loathe to admit that my husband was right. Maybe, just maybe, my story could help other people and if that was remotely possible, then I could push past my own discomfort and anxiety for the greater good. So, in May of 2015, we launched the *Colour My Life Series* in Las Vegas, Nevada. I managed to not lose my mind worrying about if anyone was going to buy ticket or show up at all.

It was a multi-media presentation complete with music, graphics, and me enthusiastically cutting and coloring hair on stage while sharing my story in the most entertaining way that I could without making a complete fool of myself. I worked hard to inspire, to motivate, and to encourage every person in the audience to push past their own boundaries, to create a vision for themselves, and to leave fear in the wind where it belonged.

The presentation was a rewarding and emotionally satisfying experience for me and I still perform portions of the series in beauty schools across the country. My goal remains to inspire everyone that I come in contact with to realize their God-given potential and to strive to be their best selves and not just in the business, but in life.

"Isaiah 40:31 – But those who hope in the Lord will renew their strength. They will soar on wings like Eagles; they will run and not grow weary, they will walk and not be faint."

Continue to make yourself better. If you are already good at what you do, you can become great at what you do!

Keep putting challenges in front of yourself.

Strive to become great. Use your talent rather than lose your talent.

Knowledge is empowering and energizing, and your clients will appreciate it!

And, as I always say, Be Open to Change!

Chapter 12

What I know for sure is to always expect the unexpected. Sometimes in life when we think everything is fine, God has a way of reminding us that our fate and our lives are always in His hands. In August of 2107, I discovered a weird bruise on my arm and elbow that wouldn't go away. I had been a little bit of a mess lately so I figured that this was just another indicator of my busy life. I had hurt my knee earlier in the year playing basketball with my boys so maybe the bruise was a result of that and I just hadn't noticed it. But if I'm to be truthful, I hadn't been feeling my best lately. I had been experiencing peculiar bouts of vertigo and my equilibrium was off. Something wasn't right. I could feel it.

I went in for a hearing test and was told that my left ear was a little below normal. Okay, I thought, I could deal with that, then the doctor suggested that I get an MRI. No one wants that suggestion. I began to panic. What if I had some golf ball-sized tumor rolling around in my head? What if? What if? I tried not to worry myself to death but it was challenging. I had an MRI and I hated every minute of it. I'm sure most people do as it is a claustrophobic and unpleasant but necessary experience.

Not too long after the test, I received a call from my doctor and he informed me that I have an eleven-millimeter lesion on the back of my brain. I was, as you can imagine, scared and horrified beyond belief. Did I have a tumor or MS or some other terminal malady that would render me bedridden, speechless, and dependent? In that moment, during that phone call, I went from 0 to "oh fuck!" in less than thirty seconds. I was going to die. My husband and the doctor assured me that I wasn't but what did they know? Did they have a lesion on the back of their brains? No. What was I supposed to do, I asked. The answer was wait another six months and get another MRI.

I was beside myself with worry. This was by far the absolute worst six months of my life. I couldn't concentrate on anything. I felt like I was walking around in slow motion. I became ill and disoriented. I developed (LPR) Laryngopharyngeal reflux, a condition similar to GERD where the contents of the stomach backs up and makes it difficult to swallow. I could barely swallow. I was a mess. My chest burned and I felt like I had a ball in my stomach every single day for six months. It seemed like I had to have bloodwork every week and ultimately, I gave myself symptoms of Multiple Sclerosis. In my neurosis, I developed asthma, I couldn't take a deep breath to save my life and I lost thirty pounds. This severe decline in my health was all due to stress. I allowed stress to nearly kill me. I realized that I was emotionally and spiritually sick. I made the decision to give my worry and my pain to God. I had to work on myself and allow him to take care of the rest. I woke up one morning and determined to live again without all of the panic and distress. I began walking and decided to play tennis for hour a week. I had to adjust my attitude, nurture my mental health or die.

Dying was not an option for me, so living was all there was left to do. Once again, it was time for me to inspire myself, this time for a challenge no one saw coming. I returned to the hospital for my follow up MRI six months later as the neurologist instructed and was told that there was no change in my brain. The lesion was still there but there was no enhancement, which in layman's terms means there was no cancer or no tumors detected. By the grace of God, my vertigo has subsided and I feel more like myself, and this is a very good thing.

Meanwhile, I had a partial tear in my ACL from fooling around with my boys on the court so I had to attend to that as well. To this date, I've had over sixty injections in my knee from my own stem cells. Every day, I'm getting better and better and every single day, I count my blessings as we all should because we only have one life to live and we've all got to make the best of it!

Having a well-developed positive culture is not just key to branding, it is also key to success and longevity in the business world.

Create a clear vision for your business or project.

When you create a strong and uplifting culture, it's easy for others to embrace it. Having a solid culture sets a standard and creates the tone for achievement.

First identify your values when creating your culture.

Next, your culture must be greater than yourself and your own ambitions. A great culture transcends, so everyone involved understands they are part of a greater mission.

Chapter 13

Today, I am the president of my own flourishing company and my life is my own. Jason and I have opened nearly 250 locations nationwide in just seven years with plans for international expansion. Phenix Salon Suites is home to more than 6000 salon professionals nationwide and our business is thriving. I, the once high school dropout, have become a seasoned columnist and my words of wisdom have been featured in over 250 publications including but not limited to *Modern Salon, Fashion & Style, Huffington Post* and *Own Magazine*. I've has been profiled on CBS, featured in Forbes Magazine, and my products have sold out in record time on the *Home Shopping Network* (HSN) on more than one occasion. Jason and I started the Priest James Foundation which supports cancer research and provide grants to salon professionals who suffer from cancer and who are in need of financial assistance. I've won awards and Phenix Salon Suites has been listed as one of the top 25 companies in Entrepreneur. I've been on the television show *EXTRA*, featured in a music video, given countless interviews and am currently shopping two shows for television.

Life has moved on in grand fashion, and I am moving forward as well, determined to be my best self for my husband, for my children, and for the salon professionals who depend on me. I've worked hard to create a business model that I could be proud of. When I have moments of doubt or when I'm struggling with anxiety about anything at all, I am comforted by the following scripture: "Have I not commanded you? Be strong and courageous. Do not be terrified. Do not be discouraged for the Lord your God will be with you wherever you go."

So, find the one thing that drives you, the thing that brings you closer to who you believe yourself to be and fight for it every single day with all of your heart. Some days will be harder than others, but that's all right; have faith in yourself and you will push through. Make mistakes and learn from them without beating yourself up. Fall, shake it off, and get back up again. Honor that voice inside that always reminds you who you are, even when you feel lost and alone. Refuse to let the truth of you stay buried underneath mistakes, bad relationships, or questionable decisions. Surround yourself with people who sincerely support you and your vision. Know that if you work hard and trust in something grander that yourself, your efforts will propel your forward and your success, no matter how big or how small, will be well worth the wait.

Understand that anxiety, failures, and frustration are a part of the journey and never allow a setback or two or three to deter you from your goal. Most importantly, when you're finally ready to realize your own vision and when you long to make sense to yourself, take my mom's sage advice and change your hair. Change can be a very good thing, my friends, Now, take a deep breath, work your plan, and be the you that you were always meant to be!

"Sometimes we don't see the big picture, we get impatient in our goals and it feels like we will never get there. The road to accomplishment can be long and every journey must begin with the first step."

Have a very clear picture or vision of what YOU want and how that want correlates to your overall mission for your life.

Next, don't let other people stop you or tell me that you can't.

Create opportunities and focus on them. Ask yourself, "what if?" rather than telling yourself "no way."

Don't put pressure on yourself for perfection right out of the gate, though perfection is something you will strive for, you will learn new things along the way and this will help you to perfect your skills.

Remember, good things come to those who wait.

Visualize your playbook before the game in order to go out and perform. If you hold true to your vision and your mission and take the proper steps without rushing, you are well on your way to achieving your goal.

So, stay focused on the vision and the mission, and get ready for the time of your life!

"1 Chronicles 4:9-10 – Jabez cried out to the God of Israel, saying, "Oh that you would bless me indeed and enlarge my territory! Let your hand be with me, and keep me from the evil one." And God granted his request."